MY FAVORITE ITALIAN

RECIPES 2021

MOUTH-WATERING TRADITIONAL AND ORIGINAL RECIPIES

SECOND EDITION (INCLUDES MANY MORE TASTY RECIPES)

PAUL LAI

BUON

APPETITO!!!

TABLE OF CONTENTS

Fillets with Tomato and Balsamic Vinegar...8

Stuffed Sole...10

Sole Rolls with Basil and Almonds..12

Marinated Tuna, Sicilian Style...14

Skewered Tuna with Orange...16

Grilled Tuna and Peppers, Molise Style...18

Grilled Tuna with Lemon and Oregano...20

Crusty Broiled Tuna Steaks..22

Seared Tuna with Arugula Pesto..24

Tuna and Cannellini Bean Stew...26

Sicilian Swordfish with Onions..28

Swordfish with Artichokes and Onions...30

Swordfish, Messina Style..32

Swordfish Rolls...34

Roasted Turbot with Vegetables..36

Pan-Fried Sea Bass with Garlicky Greens...38

Scrod with Spicy Tomato Sauce...40

Salmon Carpaccio...42

Salmon Steaks with Juniper Berries and Red Onions...44

Salmon with Spring Vegetables...46

Fish Steaks in Green Sauce 48

Halibut Baked in Paper 50

Baked Fish with Olives and Potatoes 52

Citrus Red Snapper 54

Fish in a Salt Crust 56

Roasted Fish in White Wine and Lemon..58

Trout with Prosciutto and Sage 60

Baked Sardines with Rosemary 62

Sardines, Venetian Style 64

Stuffed Sardines, Sicilian Style..66

Grilled Sardines..68

Fried Salt Cod..70

Salt Cod, Pizza Style 72

Salt Cod with Potatoes...74

Shrimp and Beans..76

Shrimp in Garlic Sauce..78

Shrimp with Tomatoes, Capers, and Lemon 80

Shrimp in Anchovy Sauce..82

Fried Shrimp...85

Batter-Fried Shrimp and Calamari 88

Grilled Shrimp Skewers 90

"Brother Devil" Lobster 92

Baked Stuffed Lobster 95

Scallops with Garlic and Parsley 97

Grilled Scallops and Shrimp 99

Clams and Mussels Posillipo 101

Baked Stuffed Clams 103

Mussels with Black Pepper 106

Mussels with Garlic and White Wine 108

Sardinian Mussels with Saffron 110

Almond Cream Cups 113

Orange Spumone 116

Almond Semifreddo 118

Florentine Frozen Dome Cake 121

Honeyed Mascarpone Sauce 124

Fresh Strawberry Sauce 125

Warm Berry Sauce 126

Year-Round Raspberry Sauce 127

Warm Chocolate Sauce 129

Ladyfingers 130

Fillets with Tomato and Balsamic Vinegar

Filleti di Pesce al Balsamico

Makes 4 servings

This combination of warm, lightly crispy fish and cool tomato-herb topping is one of my favorites.

1 large tomato, peeled, seeded, and finely chopped

2 tablespoons capers, rinsed and drained

2 tablespoons chopped fresh chives

Salt and freshly ground black pepper

1 tablespoon balsamic vinegar

¼ cup flour

1½ pounds grouper, pompano, or other firm fish fillets

4 tablespoons unsalted butter

1. Combine the tomato, capers, chives, and salt and pepper to taste. Stir in the vinegar.

2. Spread the flour on a sheet of wax paper. Sprinkle the fish with salt and pepper. Roll the fillets in the flour, lightly shaking off the excess.

3. In a large skillet, melt the butter over medium heat. Add the fish and cook, turning once, until just barely opaque when cut in the thickest part, about 8 to 10 minutes, depending on the thickness of the fillets.

4. Arrange the fillets on a serving platter. Drain the tomato mixture and spoon it over the fish. Serve hot.

Stuffed Sole

Sogliole Ripiene

Makes 4 servings

The presence of raisins, pine nuts, and capers in this tasty stuffing is normally a sign of a Sicilian dish, though this recipe comes from Liguria. Whatever its origins, the stuffing enhances plain white fish fillets. Choose large, thin fillets such as sole or flounder.

½ cup plain bread crumbs

2 tablespoons pine nuts

2 tablespoons raisins

2 tablespoons capers, rinsed and drained

1 tablespoon chopped fresh flat-leaf parsley

1 small garlic clove, finely chopped

3 tablespoons olive oil

2 tablespoons fresh lemon juice

Salt and freshly ground black pepper

4 large sole, flounder, or other thin fillets (about 1½ pounds)

1. Place a rack in the center of the oven. Preheat the oven to 400°F. Oil a large baking pan.

2. Mix together the bread crumbs, pine nuts, raisins, capers, parsley, and garlic. Add 2 tablespoons of the oil, the lemon juice, and salt and pepper to taste.

3. Set aside 2 tablespoons of the crumb mixture. Divide the remainder over half of each fillet. Fold the fillets over to enclose the filling. Arrange the fillets in the baking pan. Sprinkle with the reserved crumb mixture. Drizzle with the remaining 1 tablespoon of the oil.

4. Bake 6 to 8 minutes, or until just barely opaque when cut in the thickest part. Serve hot.

Sole Rolls with Basil and Almonds

Sogliola con Basilico e Mandorle

Makes 4 servings

Andrea Felluga of the Livio Felluga winery took my husband and me under his wing and showed us around his region of Friuli–Venezia Giulia. One memorable town we visited was Grado, on the Adriatic coast. Situated on an island, Grado was a refuge for Roman citizens of nearby Aquileia fleeing the onslaught of Attila the Hun in the fifth century. Today, it is a beach resort, though few non-Italians seem to visit, instead flocking to nearby Venice. We ate sole prepared this way at Restaurant Colussi, a lively restaurant serving typical regional food.

4 large sole, flounder, or other thin fillets (about 1½ pounds)

Salt and freshly ground black pepper

6 fresh basil leaves, finely chopped

2 tablespoons unsalted butter, melted

1 tablespoon fresh lemon juice

¼ cup sliced almonds or pine nuts

1. Place a rack in the center of the oven. Preheat the oven to 350°F. Butter a small baking dish.

2. Cut the sole fillets in half lengthwise. Place the fillets skinned-side up on a flat surface and sprinkle with salt and pepper. Sprinkle with half the basil, butter, and lemon juice. Starting at the wider end, roll up the pieces of fish. Place the rolls seam-side down in the baking dish. Drizzle with the remaining lemon juice and butter. Scatter the remaining basil and the nuts over the top.

3. Bake the fish 15 to 20 minutes, or until it is just opaque when cut in the thickest part. Serve hot.

Marinated Tuna, Sicilian Style

Tonno Condito

Makes 4 servings

The tuna in this recipe is just gently steamed, then dressed with fresh herbs and seasonings. It would make a cool and refreshing summer meal served on a bed of baby salad greens or arugula with a potato salad.

1¼ pounds tuna steaks, about ¾-inch thick

2 tablespoons red wine vinegar

Salt

3 to 4 tablespoons extra-virgin olive oil

1 garlic clove, finely chopped

2 tablespoons chopped fresh flat-leaf parsley

1 tablespoon chopped fresh mint

½ teaspoon crushed red pepper

1. Fill a pot that will fit a steamer rack with $1/2$ inch of water. Bring the water to a boil. Meanwhile, cut the tuna into $1/2$-inch-thick strips. Spread the fish on the steamer rack. Set the rack in the pot. Cover the pot and allow the tuna to steam for 3 minutes or until slightly pink in the center. Test for doneness by making a small cut in the thickest part of the fish.

2. In a deep dish, beat together the vinegar and salt. Add the oil, garlic, herbs, and crushed red pepper. Stir in the tuna pieces.

3. Let stand about 1 hour before serving.

Skewered Tuna with Orange

Spiedini di Tonno

Makes 4 servings

Every spring, Sicilian fishermen gather for la mattanza, *the tuna kill. This ritual fishing marathon involves numerous small boats filled with men that herd the migrating tuna into a series of increasingly smaller nets until they are trapped. Then the huge fish are killed and hauled aboard the boats. The process is laborious, and as the men work they sing special chants that historians date to the Middle Ages or even earlier. Though this practice is disappearing, there are still a few places along the northern and western coasts where la mattanza takes place.*

Sicilians have countless ways of cooking tuna. With this one, the aroma of the grilled orange and herbs preludes the enticing flavor of the chunks of firm-fleshed fish.

1½ pounds fresh tuna, swordfish, or salmon steaks (about 1 inch thick)

1 navel orange, cut into 16 pieces

1 small red onion, cut into 16 pieces

2 tablespoons olive oil

2 tablespoons fresh lemon juice

1 tablespoon chopped fresh rosemary

Salt and freshly ground black pepper

6 to 8 bay leaves

1. Cut the tuna into $1^1/_2$-inch chunks. In a large bowl, toss the tuna, orange, and red onion pieces with the olive oil, lemon juice, rosemary, and salt and pepper to taste.

2. Place the barbecue grill or broiler rack about 5 inches from the heat source. Preheat the grill or broiler.

3. Thread the tuna, orange pieces, onion, and bay leaves alternately on 8 skewers.

4. Broil or grill until the tuna is browned, about 3 to 4 minutes. Turn the skewers and cook until browned on the outside but still pink in the center, about 2 minutes more, or until done to taste. Serve hot.

Grilled Tuna and Peppers, Molise Style

Tonno e Peperoni

Makes 4 servings

Peppers and chiles are one of the hallmarks of Molise-style cooking. I first had this dish prepared with sgombri, *which are similar to mackerel, but I often make it with tuna steaks or swordfish.*

4 red or yellow bell peppers

4 tuna steaks (each about ¾ inch thick)

2 tablespoons olive oil

Salt and freshly ground black pepper

1 tablespoon fresh lemon juice

2 tablespoons chopped fresh flat-leaf parsley

1 small jalapeno or other fresh chile, finely chopped, or crushed red pepper to taste

1 garlic clove, finely chopped

1. Place the grill rack or broiler pan about 5 inches from the source of the heat. Prepare a medium-hot fire in a barbecue grill, or preheat the broiler.

2. Grill or broil the peppers, turning them often, until the skin is blistered and lightly charred, about 15 minutes. Place the peppers in a bowl and cover them with foil or plastic wrap.

3. Brush the tuna steaks with oil and salt and pepper to taste. Grill or broil the fish until browned on one side, about 2 minutes. Turn the fish over with tongs and cook until browned on the other side but still pink in the center, about 2 minutes more, or until done to taste. Test for doneness by making a small cut in the thickest part of the fish.

4. Core, peel, and seed the peppers. Cut the peppers into $1/2$-inch strips and place them in a bowl. Season with 2 tablespoons of the oil, the lemon juice, parsley, chile, garlic, and salt to taste. Toss gently.

5. Cut the fish into $1/2$-inch slices. Arrange the slices overlapping slightly on a serving plate. Spoon the peppers over the top. Serve warm.

Grilled Tuna with Lemon and Oregano

Tonno alla Griglia

Makes 4 servings

The first time I visited Sicily, in 1970, there weren't many restaurants; those that existed all seemed to serve the same menu. I ate either tuna or swordfish steaks prepared this way for practically every lunch and dinner. Fortunately, it was always well prepared. The Sicilians cut the fish steaks only about ½-inch thick, but I prefer them about 1-inch thick so that they do not overcook as easily. Tuna is at its best—moist and tender—when cooked until red to pink in the center, while swordfish should be just slightly pink. Because it has cartilage that needs tenderizing, shark can be cooked a little longer.

4 tuna, swordfish, or shark steaks, about 1 inch thick

Olive oil

Salt and freshly ground black pepper

1 tablespoon freshly squeezed lemon juice

½ teaspoon dried oregano

1. Place a barbecue grill or broiler rack about 5 inches away from the heat source. Preheat the grill or broiler.

2. Generously brush the steaks with the oil and add salt and pepper to taste.

3. Grill the fish until lightly browned on one side, 2 to 3 minutes. Turn the fish over and cook until lightly browned but still pink inside, about 2 minutes more, or until done to taste. Test for doneness by making a small cut in the thickest part of the fish.

4. In a small bowl, whisk together 3 tablespoons olive oil, the lemon juice, oregano, and salt and pepper to taste. Pour the lemon juice mixture over the tuna steaks and serve immediately.

Crusty Broiled Tuna Steaks

Tonno alla Griglia

Makes 4 servings

Bread crumbs make a nice crunchy coating on these fish steaks.

4 (1 inch thick) tuna or swordfish steaks

¾ cup plain dry bread crumbs

1 tablespoon chopped fresh flat-leaf parsley

1 tablespoon chopped fresh mint or 1 teaspoon dried oregano

Salt and freshly ground black pepper

4 tablespoons olive oil

Lemon wedges

1. Preheat the broiler. Oil the broiler pan. In a bowl, toss together the bread crumbs, parsley, mint, and salt and pepper to taste. Stir in 3 tablespoons of the oil, or enough to moisten the crumbs.

2. Arrange the fish steaks on the broiler pan. Scatter half of the crumbs on top of the fish, patting them in.

3. Broil the steaks about 6 inches from the flame 3 minutes, or until the crumbs are browned. Carefully turn the steaks with a metal spatula and sprinkle with the remaining crumbs. Broil 2 to 3 minutes more or until still pink in the center, or until done to taste. Test for doneness by making a small cut in the thickest part of the fish.

4. Drizzle with the remaining 1 tablespoon of oil. Serve hot, with lemon wedges.

Seared Tuna with Arugula Pesto

Tonno al Pesto

Makes 4 servings

The spicy flavor of arugula and bright emerald green color of this sauce is a perfect complement to fresh tuna or swordfish. This dish is also good at a cool room temperature.

4 tuna steaks, about 1 inch thick

Olive oil

Salt and freshly ground black pepper

Arugula Pesto

1 bunch arugula, washed and stemmed (about 2 cups lightly packed)

½ cup lightly packed fresh basil

2 garlic cloves

½ cup olive oil

Salt and freshly ground black pepper

1. Rub the fish with a little oil and salt and pepper to taste. Cover and refrigerate until ready to cook.

2. To make the pesto: In a food processor, combine the arugula, basil, and garlic and process until finely chopped. Slowly add the oil and process until smooth. Stir in salt and pepper to taste. Cover and let stand 1 hour at room temperature.

3. In a large nonstick skillet, heat 1 tablespoon oil over medium heat. Add the tuna slices and cook 2 to 3 minutes per side or until browned on the outside but still pink in the center, or until done to taste. Test for doneness by making a small cut in the thickest part of the fish.

4. Serve the tuna hot or at room temperature, drizzled with the arugula pesto.

Tuna and Cannellini Bean Stew

Stufato di Tonno

Makes 4 servings

During the winter, I tend to cook more meat than seafood because meat seems more satisfying when the weather is cold. The exception is this stew made with fresh, meaty tuna steaks and beans. It has all the rib-sticking qualities and good flavor of a bean stew but without the meat, making it perfect for people who prefer meatless meals.

2 tablespoons olive oil

1½ pounds fresh tuna (1 inch thick), cut into 1½-inch pieces

Salt and freshly ground black pepper to taste

1 large red or green bell pepper, cut into bite-size pieces

1 cup canned peeled tomatoes, drained and chopped

1 large garlic clove, finely chopped

6 fresh basil leaves, torn into bits

1 (16-ounce) can cannellini beans, rinsed and drained, or 2 cups cooked dried beans

1. Heat the oil in a large skillet over medium heat. Pat the tuna pieces dry with paper towels. When the oil is hot, add the tuna pieces without crowding the pan. Cook until the pieces are lightly browned on the outside, about 6 minutes. Transfer the tuna to a plate. Sprinkle with salt and pepper.

2. Add the bell pepper to the skillet and cook, stirring occasionally, until it begins to brown, about 10 minutes. Add the tomato, garlic, basil, and salt and pepper. Bring to a simmer. Add the beans, cover, and reduce the heat to low. Cook for 10 minutes.

3. Stir in the tuna and cook until the tuna is slightly pink in the center, about 2 minutes more, or until done to taste. Test for doneness by making a small cut in the thickest part of the fish. Serve hot.

Sicilian Swordfish with Onions

Pesce Spada a Sfinciuni

Makes 4 servings

Sicilian cooks make a mouth-watering pizza called sfinciuni, *a word that derives from the Arabic meaning "light" or "airy." The pizza has a thick yet light crust and is topped with onions, anchovies, and tomato sauce. This traditional swordfish recipe is derived from that pizza.*

3 tablespoons olive oil

1 medium onion, thinly sliced

4 anchovy fillets, chopped

1 cup peeled, seeded, and chopped fresh tomatoes, or drained and chopped canned tomatoes

Pinch of dried oregano, crumbled

Salt and freshly ground black pepper to taste

4 swordfish steaks, about ¾ inch thick

2 tablespoons plain dry bread crumbs

1. Pour 2 tablespoons of the oil into a medium skillet. Add the onion and cook until softened, about 5 minutes. Stir in the anchovies and cook 5 minutes more or until very tender. Add the tomatoes, oregano, salt, and pepper and simmer 10 minutes.

2. Place a rack in the center of the oven. Preheat the oven to 350°F. Oil a baking pan large enough to hold the fish in a single layer.

3. Pat the swordfish steaks dry. Place them in the prepared pan. Sprinkle with salt and pepper. Spoon on the sauce. Toss the bread crumbs with the remaining 1 tablespoon of the oil. Scatter the crumbs over the sauce.

4. Bake 10 minutes or until the fish is just slightly pink in the center. Test for doneness by making a small cut in the thickest part of the fish. Serve hot.

Swordfish with Artichokes and Onions

Pesce Spada con Carciofi

Makes 4 servings

Artichokes are a favorite Sicilian vegetable. They thrive in the hot, arid conditions of Sicily, and people grow them in their home gardens as a decorative plant. The Sicilian variety does not grow as large as the behemoths I sometimes see in markets here, and are much more tender.

2 medium artichokes

2 tablespoons olive oil

4 thick swordfish, tuna, or shark steaks

Salt and freshly ground black pepper

2 medium onions

4 anchovy fillets, chopped

¼ cup tomato paste

1 cup water

½ teaspoon dried oregano

1. Trim the artichokes down to the central cone of pale green leaves. With a small paring knife, peel the base and stems of the artichokes. Slice off the stem ends. Cut the artichokes in half lengthwise. Scoop out the chokes. Cut the hearts into thin slices.

2. In a large skillet, heat the oil over medium heat. Pat the swordfish dry and cook until browned on both sides, about 5 minutes. Sprinkle with salt and pepper. Remove the fish to a plate.

3. Add the onions and artichokes to the pan. Cook over medium heat, stirring frequently, until the onions are wilted, about 5 minutes. Stir in the anchovies, tomato paste, water, oregano, and salt and pepper to taste. Bring to a simmer and lower the heat. Cook 20 minutes or until the vegetables are tender, stirring occasionally.

4. Push the vegetables to the outside edge of the pan and return the fish to the skillet. Baste the fish with the sauce. Cook 1 to 2 minutes or until the fish is heated through. Serve immediately.

Swordfish, Messina Style

Pesce Spada Messinese

Makes 4 servings

Excellent swordfish is caught in the waters around Sicily, and Sicilians have countless ways to prepare it. The fish is eaten raw, sliced paper thin in a kind of carpaccio, or ground into sausages that cook in tomato sauce. Cubes of swordfish are tossed with pasta, roasted like meat, or grilled on a barbecue. This is a classic recipe from Messina, on the east coast of Sicily.

1 pound boiling potatoes

2 tablespoons olive oil

1 large onion, chopped

½ cup pitted black olives, coarsely chopped

2 tablespoons capers, rinsed and drained

2 cups peeled, seeded, and chopped tomatoes, or drained and chopped canned tomatoes

Salt and freshly ground black pepper

2 tablespoons chopped flat-leaf parsley

4 swordfish steaks, 1 inch thick

1. Scrub the potatoes and place them in a saucepan with cold
   water to cover. Bring the water to a boil and cook until the
   potatoes are tender, about 20 minutes. Drain, let cool a little,
   then peel the potatoes. Thinly slice them.

2. Pour the oil into a large saucepan. Add the onion and cook,
   stirring frequently, over medium heat until tender, about 10
   minutes. Stir in the olives, capers, and tomatoes. Season to taste
   with salt and pepper. Cook until thickened slightly, about 15
   minutes. Stir in the parsley.

3. Place a rack in the center of the oven. Preheat the oven to 425°F.
   Spoon half the sauce into a baking pan large enough to hold the
   fish in a single layer. Arrange the swordfish in the pan and
   sprinkle it with salt and pepper. Place the potatoes on top,
   overlapping the slices slightly. Spoon the remaining sauce over
   all.

4. Bake 10 minutes or until the fish is just slightly pink in the
   center and the sauce is bubbling. Serve hot.

Swordfish Rolls

Rollatini di Pesce Spada

Makes 6 servings

Like veal or chicken cutlets, very thin slices of meaty swordfish are good wrapped around a filling and cooked on a grill or broiler. Vary the filling by adding raisins, chopped olives, or pine nuts.

1½ pounds swordfish, cut into very thin slices

¾ cup plain dry bread crumbs

2 tablespoons capers, rinsed, chopped, and drained

2 tablespoons chopped fresh flat-leaf parsley

1 large garlic clove, finely chopped

Salt and freshly ground black pepper

¼ cup olive oil

2 tablespoons fresh lemon juice

1 lemon, cut into wedges

1. Place a barbecue grill or broiler rack about 5 inches away from the heat source. Preheat the grill or broiler.

2. Remove the swordfish skin. Place the slices between two sheets of plastic wrap. Gently pound the slices to an even $1/4$-inch thickness. Cut the fish into 3 × 2–inch pieces.

3. In a medium bowl, combine the bread crumbs, capers, parsley, garlic, and salt and pepper to taste. Add 3 tablespoons of the oil and mix until the crumbs are evenly moistened.

4. Place a tablespoon of the crumb mixture at one end of one piece of fish. Roll up the fish and fasten it closed with a toothpick. Place the rolls on a plate.

5. Whisk together the lemon juice and remaining oil. Brush the mixture over the rolls. Sprinkle the fish with any remaining bread crumb mixture, patting it so that it adheres.

6. Grill the rolls 3 to 4 minutes on each side, or until browned and the rolls feel firm when pressed and are lightly pink in the center. They should be slightly rare. Test for doneness by making a small cut in the thickest part of the fish. Serve hot with lemon wedges.

Roasted Turbot with Vegetables

Rombo al Forno con Verdure

Makes 4 servings

Calabria has a long coast along the Mediterranean Sea. In the summer, this region is popular with Italians and other Europeans seeking an inexpensive beach getaway. My husband and I once drove along the coast near Scalea and ate at a local restaurant with a big wood-burning oven. When we arrived, the cook was just removing big pans of vegetables roasted with olive oil and topped with fresh whitefish. The vegetables browned and infused the fish with their delicious flavor. At home, I use turbot when I can find it, but other whitefish steaks would be good too.

1 red pepper, cut into 1-inch pieces

1 medium zucchini, cut into 1-inch pieces

1 medium eggplant, cut into 1-inch pieces

4 medium boiling potatoes, cut into 1-inch pieces

1 medium onion, cut into 1-inch pieces

1 bay leaf

¼ cup plus 1 tablespoon olive oil

Salt and freshly ground black pepper

4 thick turbot, halibut, or other whitefish steaks

1 tablespoon lemon juice

2 tablespoons chopped fresh flat-leaf parsley

1. Place a rack in the center of the oven. Preheat the oven to 425°F. Choose a baking pan large enough to hold the fish and vegetables in a single layer, or use two smaller pans. In the pan combine the pepper, zucchini, eggplant, potatoes, onion, and bay leaf. Sprinkle with 1/4 cup of the olive oil and salt and pepper to taste. Toss well.

2. Bake the vegetables 40 minutes or until lightly browned and tender.

3. Put the fish steaks on a plate and sprinkle them with the remaining 1 tablespoon oil, lemon juice, parsley, and salt and pepper to taste. Push the vegetables to the outside edge of the pan and add the fish. Bake 8 to 10 minutes more, depending on the thickness of the fish, until it is just barely opaque when cut in the thickest part. Serve hot.

Pan-Fried Sea Bass with Garlicky Greens

Branzino alle Verdure

Makes 4 servings

Raisins and garlic flavoring greens such as Swiss chard, spinach, and escarole are a favorite combination from Rome on down through southern Italy. This recipe was inspired by a dish prepared by my friend, chef Mauro Mafrici, who serves the greens with crisp fried fish fillets and roasted potatoes.

1 bunch escarole (about 1 pound)

3 tablespoons olive oil

3 garlic cloves, thinly sliced

Pinch of crushed red pepper

¼ cup raisins

Salt

1¼ pounds Chilean sea bass, cod, or other firm skinless fillet, about 1½ inches thick

1. Separate the leaves and wash the escarole in several changes of cool water, paying special attention to the central white ribs where soil collects. Stack the leaves and cut them crosswise into 1-inch strips.

2. Pour 2 tablespoons of the olive oil into a large pot. Add the garlic and red pepper. Cook over medium heat until the garlic is golden, about 2 minutes.

3. Add the escarole, raisins, and a pinch of salt. Cover the pot and cook, stirring occasionally, until the escarole is tender, about 10 minutes. Taste and adjust seasoning.

4. Rinse the fish and pat dry. Sprinkle the pieces with salt and pepper. In a medium nonstick skillet, heat the remaining tablespoon of oil over medium heat. Add the fish pieces skinned-side up. Cook until the fish is golden brown, 4 to 5 minutes. Cover the pan and cook 2 to 3 minutes more, or until the fish is just barely opaque in the center. Test for doneness by making a small cut in the thickest part of the fish. There is no need to turn the fish.

5. With a slotted spoon, transfer the escarole to 4 serving plates. Top with the fish browned-side up. Serve hot.

Scrod with Spicy Tomato Sauce

Merluzzo in Salsa di Pomodoro

Makes 4 servings

We ate this fish at the home of Neapolitan friends, accompanied by Falanghina, a delicious white wine from the region. Couscous goes well with the fish.

2 tablespoons olive oil

1 medium onion, thinly sliced

Pinch of crushed red pepper

2 cups canned tomatoes with their juice, chopped

Pinch of dried oregano, crumbled

Salt

1¼ pounds scrod or grouper fillets, cut into serving pieces

½ teaspoon grated lemon zest

1. Pour the oil into a medium skillet. Add the onion and red pepper. Cook, stirring often, over medium heat, until the onion is tender and golden, about 10 minutes. Add the tomatoes, oregano, and salt and simmer until the sauce is thickened, about 15 minutes.

2. Rinse the fish and pat dry, then sprinkle it with salt. Add the fish to the pan and baste it with the sauce. Cover and cook 8 to 10 minutes, depending on the thickness of the fish, until it is just barely opaque when cut in the thickest part.

3. With a slotted spoon, transfer the fish to a serving platter. If the fish has released a lot of liquid, raise the heat under the pan and cook, stirring frequently, until the sauce is thickened.

4. Remove the sauce from the heat and stir in the lemon zest. Spoon the sauce over the fish and serve immediately.

Salmon Carpaccio

Carpaccio di Salmone

Makes 4 servings

Usually, carpaccio *refers to paper-thin slices of raw beef served with a creamy pink sauce. The recipe was supposedly created about a hundred years ago by a Venetian restaurateur who wanted to pamper a favorite client whose doctor had advised her to avoid eating cooked food. The restaurateur named the dish after Vittore Carpaccio, a painter whose work was on exhibit at the time.*

Today the term carpaccio is applied to thinly sliced foods both raw and cooked. These thin salmon cutlets are cooked on only one side so that they stay moist and keep their shape.

4 cups watercress

3 tablespoons extra-virgin olive oil

1 tablespoon fresh lemon juice

$\frac{1}{2}$ teaspoon grated lemon zest

Salt and freshly ground black pepper

1 pound salmon fillet, cut into thin slices like cutlets

1 green onion, finely chopped

1. Rinse the watercress in several changes of cool water. Remove the tough stems and dry the leaves thoroughly. Tear into bite-size pieces and place them in a bowl.

2. In a bowl, whisk together 2 tablespoons of oil, lemon juice, zest, and salt and pepper to taste.

3. Heat 1 tablespoon oil in a large nonstick skillet over high heat. Add just enough fish as will fit in a single layer. Cook until lightly browned on the bottom, yet still rare on top, about 1 minute. With a large spatula, remove the salmon from the skillet and turn it browned-side up onto a large serving platter. Sprinkle with salt and pepper to taste and half of the green onion. Cook the remaining salmon in the same way and add it to the platter. Top with the remaining onion.

4. Toss the watercress with the dressing. Pile the salad on top of the salmon. Serve immediately.

Salmon Steaks with Juniper Berries and Red Onions

Salmone al Ginepro

Makes 4 servings

Juniper berries are the typical flavoring in gin and are often used to spice up stews made with game. You can find them in many markets that sell gourmet spices. In this salmon dish, which I first ate in Venice, sweet red onions and juniper are cooked until the onions are meltingly soft and become a sauce for the salmon.

3 tablespoons olive oil

4 salmon steaks, about ¾ inch thick

Salt and freshly ground black pepper

2 medium red onions, thinly sliced

½ teaspoon juniper berries

½ cup dry white wine

1. In a medium skillet, heat the oil over medium heat. Pat the salmon steaks dry and place them in the pan. Cook until browned, about 3 minutes. Turn the salmon steaks and brown on the other side, about 2 minutes more. With a spatula, remove the steaks to a plate. Sprinkle with salt and pepper.

2. Add the onions, juniper berries, and salt to taste to the pan. Add the wine and bring to a simmer. Lower the heat and cover the pan. Cook 20 minutes or until the onions are soft.

3. Return the salmon steaks to the pan and spoon the onions over the fish. Turn the heat to medium. Cover and cook about 2 minutes more or until the fish is just barely opaque when cut in the thickest part. Serve immediately.

Salmon with Spring Vegetables

Salmone Primavera

Makes 4 servings

*Salmon is not a Mediterranean fish, but a lot of it has been imported
to Italy from northern Europe in recent years, and it has become
very popular in Italian kitchens. This recipe of roasted salmon with
spring vegetables was a special dish at a restaurant in Milan.*

*Vary the vegetables, but be sure to use a very large pan so that they
can be spread out in a shallow layer. If they are too crowded, the
vegetables will get soggy instead of browned. I use a 15 × 10 × 1–
inch jelly roll pan. If you don't have one large enough, divide the
ingredients between two smaller pans.*

4 medium red or white waxy potatoes

1 cup peeled and trimmed baby carrots

8 whole shallots or 2 small onions, peeled

3 tablespoons olive oil

Salt and freshly ground black pepper

8 ounces asparagus, cut into 2-inch lengths

4 salmon steaks

2 tablespoons chopped fresh herbs, such as chives, dill, parsley, basil, or a combination

1. Place a rack in the center of the oven. Preheat the oven to 425°F. Cut the potatoes into thick slices and pat them dry. In a large roasting pan, combine the potatoes, carrots, and shallots or onions. Add the oil and salt and pepper to taste. Toss well. Spread the vegetables in the pan and bake for 20 minutes.

2. Stir the vegetables and add the asparagus. Bake 10 minutes more or until the vegetables are lightly browned.

3. Sprinkle the salmon with salt and pepper. Push the vegetables to the sides of the pan. Add the salmon steaks. Bake 7 minutes more or until the salmon is just barely opaque and still moist when cut in the thickest part. Sprinkle with the herbs and serve immediately.

Fish Steaks in Green Sauce

Pesce in Salsa Verde

Makes 4 servings

I spent New Year's Eve in Venice with friends one year, and before going to the midnight services at St. Mark's Cathedral, we had dinner at a little trattoria near the Rialto Bridge. We ate grilled prawns, risotto with cuttlefish, and this dish of sautéed fish steaks in a parsley and white wine sauce with peas. After dinner, we walked through the streets, which were filled with good-natured revelers, many wearing fabulous costumes.

½ cup all-purpose flour

Salt and freshly ground black pepper

4 halibut, tilefish, or other white fish steaks, about 1 inch thick

4 tablespoons olive oil

4 green onions, finely chopped

¾ cup dry white wine

¼ cup chopped fresh flat-leaf parsley

1 cup fresh or frozen baby peas

1. On a piece of wax paper, combine the flour and salt and pepper to taste. Rinse the fish and pat dry, then dredge each steak in the flour mixture to lightly coat both sides. Shake off the excess.

2. In a large skillet, heat 2 tablespoons of the oil over medium heat. Add the fish and brown on one side, about 3 minutes. Turn the fish and brown the other side, about 2 minutes. With a slotted metal spatula, transfer the steaks to a plate. Wipe out the skillet.

3. Pour the remaining 2 tablespoons oil into the skillet. Add the onions. Cook over medium heat until golden, about 10 minutes. Add the wine and bring to a simmer. Cook until most of the liquid is evaporated, about 1 minute. Stir in the parsley.

4. Return the fish to the skillet and baste it with the sauce. Scatter the peas around the fish. Reduce the heat to low. Cover and cook 5 to 7 minutes or until the fish is just barely opaque when cut in the thickest part. Serve immediately.

Halibut Baked in Paper

Pesce in Cartoccio

Makes 4 servings

Fish baked in a parchment paper package is a dramatic dish that is actually quite easy to make. The paper holds in all of the flavor of the fish and seasonings and has the added advantage of saving on clean up. Aluminum foil can be substituted for the parchment, but it is not as attractive.

2 medium tomatoes, seeded and chopped

2 green onions, finely chopped

¼ teaspoon dried marjoram or thyme

2 tablespoons fresh lemon juice

2 tablespoons olive oil

Salt and freshly ground black pepper

4 (6-ounce) halibut, salmon, or other fish steaks, about 1-inch thick

1. Place a rack in the center of the oven. Preheat the oven to 400°F. In a medium bowl, mix together all of the ingredients except the fish.

2. Cut 4 sheets of parchment paper into 12-inch squares. Fold each sheet in half. Open the paper and brush the inside with oil. Place a fish steak to one side of the crease. Spoon the tomato mixture over the fish.

3. Fold the paper over the fish. Seal each package by making small folds from one end to the other all along the edges and creasing firmly. Carefully slide the packages onto 2 baking sheets.

4. Bake 12 minutes. To check for doneness, slit one package and cut the fish in the thickest part. It should be just barely opaque.

5. Slide the packages onto serving plates and allow the diners to open their own. Serve hot.

Baked Fish with Olives and Potatoes

Pesce al Forno

Makes 4 servings

Marjoram is an herb that is used often in Liguria, though it is not very well known in the United States. It has a flavor similar to oregano, though it is much less assertive than dried oregano. Thyme is a good substitute.

Start the potatoes ahead of time so that they get a chance to brown and cook thoroughly. Then add the fish so that everything bakes together in perfect harmony. A green salad is all you need to follow.

2 pounds boiling potatoes, peeled and thinly sliced

6 tablespoons olive oil

Salt and freshly ground black pepper to taste

2 tablespoons chopped fresh flat-leaf parsley

$\frac{1}{2}$ teaspoon dried marjoram or thyme

2 tablespoons fresh lemon juice

$\frac{1}{2}$ teaspoon freshly grated lemon zest

2 whole fish such as red snapper or sea bass (about 2 pounds each), cleaned with heads and tails intact

½ cup mild black olives, such as Gaeta

1. Place a rack in the center of the oven. Preheat the oven to 450°F. In a large bowl, toss the potatoes with 3 tablespoons of the oil and salt and pepper to taste. Spread the potatoes in a large shallow roasting pan. Bake the potatoes 25 to 30 minutes, or until they begin to turn brown.

2. Stir together the remaining 3 tablespoons of the oil, the parsley, marjoram, lemon juice, zest, and salt and pepper to taste. Place half of the mixture inside the cavity of the fish and rub the remainder over the skin.

3. With a large spatula, turn the potatoes and scatter the olives all around. Rinse the fish well and pat dry. Place the fish on top of the potatoes. Bake about 8 to 10 minutes per inch of thickness at the widest point of the fish, or until the flesh is opaque when cut with a small sharp knife near the bone and the potatoes are tender.

4. Transfer the fish to a warm serving platter. Surround the fish with the potatoes and olives. Serve immediately.

Citrus Red Snapper

Pesce al Agrumi

Makes 4 servings

No matter what the weather is outside, you will feel like it is a glorious sunny day when you serve this fish roasted with citrus fruits. The recipe is based on one I tasted in Positano. A crisp, fresh wine such as pinot grigio is the perfect accompaniment.

1 medium orange

1 medium lemon

2 whole fish such as red snapper or sea bass (about 2 pounds each), cleaned with heads and tails intact

2 teaspoons chopped fresh thyme leaves

2 tablespoons olive oil

Salt and freshly ground black pepper

½ cup dry white wine

1 orange and 1 lemon, sliced, for garnish

1. With a swivel-blade vegetable peeler, remove half of the zest from the orange and lemon skin. Stack the pieces and cut them into narrow strips. Squeeze the fruits to extract the juice.

2. Place a rack in the center of the oven. Preheat the oven to 400°F. Oil a baking pan large enough to hold the fish in a single layer.

3. Rinse the fish well and pat dry. Place the fish in the pan and stuff the cavity with the thyme and half the zest. Sprinkle inside and out with the oil and salt and pepper to taste. Pour the wine, juice, and remaining zest over the fish.

4. Bake, basting once or twice with the pan juices, about 8 to 10 minutes per inch of thickness at the widest point of the fish, or until the flesh is opaque when cut with a small sharp knife near the bone. Serve hot, garnished with orange and lemon slices.

Fish in a Salt Crust

Pesce in Sale

Makes 2 servings

Fish and seafood baked in salt is a traditional dish in Liguria and along the Tuscan coast. Mixed with egg white, the salt forms a thick hard crust so that the fish inside cooks in its own juices. At Baia Beniamin, a beautiful restaurant right on the water in Ventimiglia near the French border, I watched as the waiter deftly cracked the salt crust with the back of a heavy spoon and lifted it away, removing the skin and salt in one motion. Inside, the fish was cooked to perfection.

6 cups kosher salt

4 large egg whites

1 whole fish such as red snapper or sea bass (about 2 pounds each), cleaned with head and tail intact

1 tablespoon chopped fresh rosemary

2 garlic cloves, finely chopped

1 lemon, cut into wedges

Extra-virgin olive oil

1. Place a rack in the center of the oven. Preheat the oven to 500°F. In a large bowl, stir together the salt and egg whites until the salt is evenly moistened.

2. Oil a baking sheet large enough to hold the fish. Place the fish on the baking sheet. Stuff the cavity with the rosemary and garlic.

3. Mound the salt evenly on the fish, covering it completely. Pat the salt firmly so it will hold.

4. Bake the fish 30 minutes or until the salt is beginning to turn lightly golden around the edges. To test for doneness, insert an instant-read thermometer through the salt into the thickest part of the fish. The fish is done when the temperature reaches 130°F.

5. To serve, crack the salt crust with a large spoon. Lift the salt and skin away from the fish and discard. Carefully lift the flesh away from the bones. Serve hot with the lemon wedges and a drizzle of extra-virgin olive oil.

Roasted Fish in White Wine and Lemon

Pesce al Vino Bianco

Makes 4 servings

This is a basic way to cook any medium to small whole fish. I had this in Liguria, where it was accompanied by braised artichokes and potatoes.

2 whole fish such as red snapper or sea bass (about 2 pounds each), cleaned with heads and tails intact

1 tablespoon chopped fresh rosemary

Salt and freshly ground black pepper

1 lemon, thinly sliced

2 tablespoons chopped fresh flat-leaf parsley

1 cup dry white wine

1/4 cup extra-virgin olive oil

1 tablespoon white wine vinegar

1. Place a rack in the center of the oven. Preheat the oven to 400°F. Oil a pan large enough to hold the fish side by side.

2. Rinse the fish and pat dry inside and out. Sprinkle the insides of the fish with the rosemary and salt and pepper to taste. Tuck some of the lemon slices inside the cavity. Place the fish in the pan. Scatter the parsley over the fish and lay the remaining lemon slices on top. Drizzle with the wine, oil, and vinegar.

3. Bake the fish 8 to 10 minutes per inch of thickness at the widest point, or until the flesh is opaque when cut with a small sharp knife near the bone. Serve hot.

Trout with Prosciutto and Sage

Trote al Prosciutto e Salvia

Makes 4 servings

Wild trout is very flavorful, though it is rarely found in fish markets. Farm-raised trout is a lot less interesting, but prosciutto and sage enhance the flavor. I had trout prepared this way in Friuli–Venezia Giulia, where it was made with the local prosciutto from the town of San Daniele.

4 small whole trout, cleaned, about 12 ounces each

4 tablespoons olive oil

2 to 3 tablespoons fresh lemon juice

6 fresh sage leaves, finely chopped

Salt and freshly ground black pepper

8 very thin slices imported Italian prosciutto

1 lemon, cut into wedges

1. Oil a baking pan large enough to hold the fish in a single layer.

2. In a small bowl, combine the oil, lemon juice, sage, and salt and pepper to taste. Sprinkle the fish inside and out with the mixture. Marinate the fish in the refrigerator for 1 hour.

3. Place the oven rack in the center of the oven. Preheat the oven to 375°F. Place a slice of prosciutto inside each fish and lay another slice on top. Bake 20 minutes or until the fish is just opaque when cut with a small sharp knife near the bone. Serve hot with lemon wedges.

Baked Sardines with Rosemary

Sarde con Rosamarina

Makes 4 servings

Sardines, smelts, and anchovies belong to the family of dark-fleshed fish known in Italy as pesce azzurro. *Other members of this family include mackerel and, of course, bluefish. Rosemary complements them nicely in this recipe from Tuscany.*

1½ pounds fresh sardines, smelts, or anchovies, cleaned (see Note below)

Salt and freshly ground black pepper

1 tablespoon chopped fresh rosemary

¼ cup olive oil

¼ cup plain fine dry bread crumbs

1 lemon, cut into wedges

1. Place the rack in the center of the oven. Preheat the oven to 400°F. Oil a baking dish large enough to hold the sardines in a single layer.

2. Place the sardines in the dish and sprinkle inside and out with salt, pepper, and rosemary. Drizzle with the oil and sprinkle with bread crumbs.

3. Bake 15 minutes or until the fish are cooked through. Serve with lemon wedges.

> ***Note:*** *To clean sardines: With a large heavy chef's knife or kitchen shears, cut off the heads. Slit the fish open along the belly and remove the innards. Pull out the backbone. Snip off the fins. Rinse and drain.*

Sardines, Venetian Style

Sarde in Saor

Makes 4 servings

Raisins and vinegar give a delicious sweet-and-sour flavor to fish in this Venetian classic. Be sure to make this recipe at least a day before you plan to serve it so that the flavors can mellow. Small portions are excellent as an appetizer. Whole trout or mackerel can be substituted for the sardines, or try sole fillets. In Venice, sarde in saor *is often served with grilled white* <u>Polenta</u>.

8 tablespoons olive oil

3 onions (about 1 pound), sliced $\frac{1}{2}$ inch thick

1 cup dry white wine

1 cup white wine vinegar

2 tablespoons pine nuts

2 tablespoons raisins

2 pounds sardines, cleaned

1. Pour 4 tablespoons of oil into a large heavy skillet. Add the onions and cook over medium-low heat until very tender, about 20 minutes. Stir frequently and watch carefully so that the onions do not brown. Add a tablespoon or two of water if needed to prevent the onions from coloring.

2. Add $1/2$ cup of wine, $1/2$ cup of vinegar, the raisins, and the pine nuts. Bring to a simmer and cook 1 minute. Remove from the heat.

3. In another skillet, heat the remaining 4 tablespoons oil over medium heat. Add the sardines and cook until just opaque in the center, about 2 to 3 minutes per side. Arrange the sardines in a single layer on a large platter. Pour on the remaining wine and vinegar.

4. Spread the onion mixture over the fish. Cover and refrigerate 1 to 2 days to allow the flavors to mellow. Serve at cool room temperature.

Stuffed Sardines, Sicilian Style

Sarde Beccafico

Makes 4 servings

Dr. Joseph Maniscalco, an old family friend who came from Sciacca in Sicily, taught me how to make this typically Sicilian recipe. The Italian name means sardines in the style of a figpecker, a succulent little bird that loves to eat ripe figs.

1 cup plain dry bread crumbs

About ¼ cup olive oil

4 anchovy fillets, drained and chopped

2 tablespoons chopped fresh flat-leaf parsley

2 tablespoons pine nuts

2 tablespoons raisins

Salt and freshly ground black pepper

2 pounds fresh sardines, cleaned

Bay leaves

Lemon wedges

1. Place a rack in the center of the oven. Preheat the oven to 375°F. Oil a small baking pan.

2. In a large skillet, toast the bread crumbs over medium heat, stirring constantly, until browned. Remove from the heat and stir in just enough oil to moisten them. Add the anchovies, parsley, pine nuts, raisins, and salt and pepper to taste. Mix well.

3. Open the sardines like a book and place them skin side down on a flat surface. Spoon a little of the bread crumb mixture at the head end of each sardine. Roll up the sardines, enclosing the filling, and place them side by side in the pan, separating each with a bay leaf. Sprinkle any remaining crumbs over the top and drizzle with the remaining oil.

4. Bake 20 minutes or until the rolls are just cooked through. Serve hot or at room temperature with lemon wedges.

Grilled Sardines

Sarde alla Griglia

Makes 4 servings

Small, tasty fish like sardines, smelts, and anchovies are irresistible when cooked on the grill. At a barbecue dinner at a winery in Abruzzo, the guests arrived to find rows and rows of the little fish cooking over a charcoal fire. Though it looked like there were too many, they soon disappeared, washed down with glasses of chilled white trebbiano wine.

A basket grill does a good job of holding and turning the little fish as they cook. If you are fortunate enough to grow your own lemon or orange trees and they have not been treated with chemicals, use some of the leaves to garnish the serving platter. Otherwise, radicchio or firm lettuce leaves will do.

12 to 16 fresh sardines or smelts, cleaned

2 tablespoons olive oil

Salt and freshly ground black pepper

Untreated lemon leaves or radicchio

2 lemons, cut into wedges

1. Place a barbecue grill or broiler rack about 5 inches away from the heat source. Preheat a barbecue grill or broiler.

2. Pat the sardines dry and brush with the oil. Sprinkle lightly with salt and pepper. Grill or broil the fish until nicely browned, about 3 minutes. Gently turn the fish over and cook until browned on the other side, about 2 to 3 minutes more.

3. Arrange the leaves on a platter. Top with the sardines and garnish with the lemon wedges. Serve hot.

Fried Salt Cod

Baccala Fritta

Makes 4 servings

This is a basic recipe for cooking baccala. It can be served plain or topped with tomato sauce. Some cooks like to heat the sauce in a skillet and then add the fried fish, simmering them together briefly.

About 1 cup all-purpose flour

Salt and freshly ground black pepper

1 pound soaked baccala or stockfish, cut into serving pieces

Olive oil

Lemon wedges

1. Spread the flour and salt and pepper to taste on a piece of wax paper.

2. In a large heavy skillet, heat about $1/2$ inch of the oil. Quickly dip the fish pieces in the flour mixture, lightly shaking off the excess. Place as many fish pieces in the pan as will fit without crowding.

3. Cook the fish until browned, 2 to 3 minutes. Turn the fish with tongs, then cook until browned and tender, 2 to 3 minutes more. Serve hot with lemon wedges.

Variation: Add lightly crushed whole garlic cloves and/or fresh or dried chile peppers to the frying oil to flavor the fish.

Salt Cod, Pizza Style

Baccala alla Pizzaiola

Makes 6 to 8 servings 8

In Naples, tomatoes, garlic, and oregano are the typical flavors of a classic pizza sauce, so this dish flavored with those ingredients is called pizza-style. For extra flavor, add a handful of olives and a few anchovy fillets to the sauce.

2 pounds soaked salt cod, cut into serving pieces

4 tablespoons olive oil

2 large garlic cloves, very finely chopped

2 tablespoons chopped fresh flat-leaf parsley

Pinch of crushed red pepper

3 cups peeled, seeded, and chopped fresh tomatoes, or 1 (28-ounce) can Italian peeled tomatoes, drained and chopped

2 tablespoons capers, rinsed, drained, and chopped

1 teaspoon dried oregano, crumbled

Salt

1. Bring about 2 inches of water to a simmer in a deep skillet. Add the fish and cook until the fish is tender but does not break apart, about 10 minutes. Remove the fish with a slotted spoon and drain.

2. Pour the oil into a large skillet with the garlic, parsley, and crushed red pepper. Cook until the garlic is lightly golden, about 2 minutes. Add the tomatoes and their juice, the capers, oregano, and a tiny bit of salt. Bring to a simmer and cook until the liquid is slightly thickened, about 15 minutes.

3. Add the drained fish. Baste the fish with the sauce. Cook 10 minutes or until just tender. Serve hot.

Salt Cod with Potatoes

Baccala Palermitana

Makes 4 servings

A stroll through the Vucciria market in Palermo, Sicily, is a fascinating experience for anyone, especially a cook. The market stands line the crowded, winding streets, and shoppers can select from a range of fresh meat, fish, and produce (as well as anything from underwear to batteries). Fishmongers sell baccala and stockfish already soaked and ready to cook. Here in the United States, if you don't have the time to soak the fish, substitute chunks of fresh cod or another firm whitefish for the baccala.

1/4 cup olive oil

1 medium onion, sliced

1 cup chopped canned tomatoes with their juice

1/2 cup chopped celery

2 medium potatoes, peeled and sliced

1 1/2 pounds baccala, soaked and drained

1/4 cup chopped green olives

1. In a large skillet, heat the oil over medium heat. Add the onion, tomatoes, celery, and potatoes. Bring to a simmer and cook until the potatoes are tender, about 20 minutes.

2. Add the fish and baste the pieces with the sauce. Sprinkle with the olives. Cook until the fish is tender, about 10 minutes. Taste for seasoning and add salt if needed. Serve hot.

Shrimp and Beans

Gamberi e Fagioli

Makes 4 servings

Forte dei Marmi is a beautiful town on the Tuscan coast. It has an old-world elegance, with many Art Deco palazzos, some of which have been converted into hotels. Along the beach you can rent a lounge chair and an umbrella for a day, a week, or a month. My husband and I, with friends Rob and Linda Leahy, had a long discussion about whether to spend a day on the beach or eat at a restaurant called Lorenzo. Linda decided to soak up the sun while the rest of us went to the restaurant, which specializes in simple seafood preparations, like these shrimp. We were glad we did.

16 to 20 large shrimp, peeled and deveined

4 tablespoons olive oil

2 tablespoons finely chopped fresh garlic

2 tablespoons chopped fresh basil

Salt and freshly ground black pepper

3 cups drained cooked or canned cannellini or Great Northern beans

2 medium tomatoes, diced

Fresh basil leaves, for garnish

1. In a bowl, drizzle the shrimp with 2 tablespoons of the oil, half the garlic, 1 tablespoon of the basil, and salt and pepper to taste. Stir well. Cover and refrigerate 1 hour.

2. Place a barbecue grill or broiler rack about 5 inches away from the heat source. Preheat the grill or broiler.

3. In a saucepan, cook the remaining oil, garlic, and basil over medium heat about 1 minute. Stir in the beans. Cover and cook over low heat 5 minutes or until heated through. Remove from the heat. Stir in the tomatoes, and salt and pepper to taste.

4. Broil the shrimp on one side until lightly browned, 1 to 2 minutes. Turn the shrimp and cook until lightly browned and just opaque in the thickest part, about 1 to 2 minutes more.

5. Spoon the beans onto 4 plates. Arrange the shrimp around the beans. Garnish with fresh basil leaves. Serve immediately.

Shrimp in Garlic Sauce

Gamberi al'Aglio

Makes 4 to 6 servings

Shrimp cooked in a garlicky butter sauce is more popular in Italian-American restaurants than it is in Italy. It is often called "shrimp scampi" here, a nonsensical name that is a clue to its non-Italian origins. Scampi is not, as the name implies, a style of cooking but a type of shellfish that looks a lot like a miniature lobster. As for cooking them, scampi are generally grilled with nothing more than a little olive oil, parsley, and lemon.

Whatever you call it, and whatever its origins, shrimp in garlic sauce is delicious. Offer lots of good bread to soak up the sauce.

6 tablespoons unsalted butter

¼ cup olive oil

4 large garlic cloves, finely chopped

16 to 24 large shrimp, peeled and deveined

Salt

3 tablespoons chopped fresh flat-leaf parsley

2 tablespoons fresh lemon juice

1. In a large skillet, melt the butter with the olive oil over medium heat. Stir in the garlic. Cook until the garlic is lightly golden, about 2 minutes.

2. Turn up the heat to medium-high. Add the shrimp, and salt to taste. Cook 1 to 2 minutes, turn the shrimp once, and cook until they are just pink, about 1 to 2 minutes more. Stir in the parsley and lemon juice and cook 1 minute more. Serve hot.

Shrimp with Tomatoes, Capers, and Lemon

Gamberi in Salsa

Makes 4 servings

This is one of those quick, adaptable recipes that Italians do so well. Serve it as is for a speedy shrimp main dish, or toss it with pasta and some extra-virgin olive oil for a hearty meal.

2 tablespoons olive oil

1 pound medium shrimp, peeled and deveined

1 garlic clove, lightly smashed

Salt

1 pint grape or cherry tomatoes, halved or quartered if large

2 tablespoons capers, rinsed and drained

2 tablespoons chopped fresh flat-leaf parsley

¼ teaspoon grated lemon zest

1. In a 10-inch skillet, heat the oil over medium-high heat. Add the shrimp, garlic, and a pinch of salt. Cook until the shrimp turn

pink and lightly golden, about 1 to 2 minutes per side. Transfer the shrimp to a plate.

2. Add the tomatoes and capers to the pan. Cook, stirring frequently, until the tomatoes are slightly softened, about 2 minutes. Return the shrimp to the pan and add the parsley and salt to taste. Stir well and cook 2 minutes more.

3. Add the lemon zest. Discard the garlic and serve immediately.

Shrimp in Anchovy Sauce

Gamberi in Salsa di Acciughe

Makes 4 servings

One spring, the Gruppo Ristoratori Italiani, an organization of
Italian restaurateurs in the United States, asked me to join them and
a group of other food writers on a trip to the Marche region of
central Italy. We stayed at a hotel on the coast and planned to take
trips to explore the surrounding towns. One night, stormy weather
made traveling all but impossible, so we ate at a local restaurant
called Tre Nodi. The owner was a little eccentric and lectured us on
his theories about politics, food, and cooking, but the seafood was
wonderful, especially the big red Mediterranean shrimp cooked with
anchovies. The shrimp were split nearly in half, then opened flat so
that they could be coated thoroughly with the sauce. When we left,
the owner gave each of us a small container of sand from the local
beach to remind us of our stay.

1½ pounds jumbo shrimp

4 tablespoons unsalted butter

3 tablespoons olive oil

2 tablespoons chopped fresh flat-leaf parsley

2 large garlic cloves, very finely chopped

6 anchovy fillets, chopped

⅓ cup dry white wine

2 tablespoons fresh lemon juice

Salt and freshly ground black pepper

1. Peel the shrimp, leaving the tail sections intact. With a small knife, slit the shrimp lengthwise along the back, cutting almost all the way through to the other side. Remove the dark vein and open the shrimp flat like a book. Rinse the shrimp and pat dry.

2. Place a barbecue grill or broiler rack about 5 inches away from the heat source. Preheat the grill or broiler. In a large broiler-safe skillet, melt the butter with the olive oil over medium heat. When the butter foam subsides, add the parsley, garlic, and anchovies and cook, stirring 1 minute. Add the wine and lemon juice and cook 1 minute more.

3. Remove the skillet from the heat. Add the shrimp cut-sides down. Sprinkle with salt and pepper. Spoon some of the sauce over the shrimp.

4. Run the pan under the broiler and cook about 3 minutes or until the shrimp are just opaque. Serve immediately.

Fried Shrimp

Gamberi Fritti

Makes 4 to 6 servings

A simple flour-and-water batter makes a delicious crispy crust for fried shrimp. Note that this type of batter will not brown much because it has no sugars or protein. For a deeper brown crust, try the beer batter (Fried Zucchini, step 2) or one made with eggs, such as in the Batter-Fried Shrimp and Calamari recipe. Another trick used by many restaurant chefs is to add a tablespoon of cooking oil left from the previous day's frying to the pot. The reasons are complicated, but if you deep-fry a lot, it is worthwhile to keep some of the cooled leftover oil strained and refrigerated for the next time you fry. It does not keep indefinitely, however, and you should always smell the oil before using it to be sure that it is still fresh.

Serve these shrimp as a main dish or appetizer. If you like, whole green beans, strips of zucchini or peppers, or other vegetables can be fried in the same way. Also good are whole parsley, basil, or sage leaves.

1 cup all-purpose flour

1½ teaspoons salt

About ¾ cup cold water

1½ pounds medium shrimp, shelled and deveined

Vegetable oil for frying

1. Put the flour and salt in a medium bowl. Gradually add the
   water, stirring with a wire whisk until smooth. The mixture
   should be very thick, like sour cream.

2. Rinse the shrimp and pat them dry. Line a tray with paper
   towels.

3. In a deep heavy saucepan, pour enough oil to reach a depth of 2
   inches, or if using an electric deep-fryer, follow the
   manufacturer's directions. Heat the oil to 370°F. on a frying
   thermometer or until a drop of the batter placed in the oil sizzles
   and browns in 1 minute.

4. Place the shrimp in the bowl with the batter and stir to coat.
   Remove the shrimp one at a time and with tongs carefully place
   them in the oil. Fry at one time only as many shrimp as will fit
   without crowding. Cook the shrimp until very lightly golden and
   crisp, 1 to 2 minutes. Drain on the paper towels. Fry the

remaining shrimp in the same way. Serve hot with lemon wedges.

Batter-Fried Shrimp and Calamari

Frutti di Mare in Pastella

Makes 6 servings

Wherever you find seafood in Italy, you will find cooks frying it in a crispy batter. This batter is made with eggs and yeast, which gives the crust a light, airy texture, golden color, and good flavor. Though I use olive oil for most cooking purposes, I prefer a tasteless vegetable oil for frying.

1 teaspoon active dry yeast or instant yeast

1 cup warm water (100 to 110°F)

2 large eggs

1 cup all-purpose flour

1 teaspoon salt

1 pound small shrimp, shelled and deveined

8 ounces cleaned calamari (squid)

Vegetable oil for frying

1 lemon, cut into wedges

1. In a medium bowl, sprinkle the yeast over the water. Let stand 1 minute or until creamy. Stir to dissolve.

2. Add the eggs to the yeast mixture and beat well. Stir in the flour and salt. Beat with a whisk until smooth.

3. Rinse the shrimp and calamari well. Pat dry. Cut the calamari crosswise into $1/2$-inch rings. If large, cut the base of each group of tentacles in half.

4. In a deep heavy saucepan, pour enough oil to reach a depth of 2 inches, or if using an electric deep-fryer, follow the manufacturer's directions. Heat the oil to 370°F. on a frying thermometer or until a drop of the batter placed in the oil sizzles and browns in 1 minute.

5. Stir the shrimp and calamari into the batter. Remove the pieces a few at a time, letting the excess batter drip back into the bowl. Very carefully place the pieces in the hot oil. Do not crowd the pan. Fry, stirring once with a slotted spoon, until golden brown, 1 to 2 minutes. Remove the seafood from the pan and drain on paper towels. Fry the remainder in the same way. Serve hot with lemon wedges.

Grilled Shrimp Skewers

Spiedini di Gamberi

Makes 4 servings

Though the rich cooking of Parma and Bologna is better known, the cooking of coastal Emilia-Romagna is very good and often very simple. Excellent fruits and vegetables from area farms and wonderful fresh seafood are the mainstays. My husband and I ate these grilled shrimp skewers in the beach town of Milano Marittima. Chunks of firm-fleshed fish can be substituted for the shellfish.

½ cup plain bread crumbs

1 tablespoon finely chopped fresh rosemary

1 garlic clove, peeled and finely chopped

Salt and freshly ground black pepper

2 tablespoons olive oil

1 pound medium shrimp, peeled and deveined

1 lemon, cut into wedges

1. Place a barbecue grill or broiler rack about 5 inches away from the heat source. Preheat the grill or broiler.

2. In a medium bowl, combine the bread crumbs, rosemary, garlic, salt and pepper to taste, and oil and mix well. Add the shrimp and stir to coat well. Thread the shrimp on skewers.

3. Grill or broil until the shrimp are pink and cooked through, about 3 minutes on each side. Serve hot with lemon wedges.

"Brother Devil" Lobster

Aragosta Fra Diavolo

Makes 2 to 4 servings

Though this recipe has many of the characteristics of a classic southern Italian seafood dish, including the tomatoes, garlic, and hot pepper, I have always suspected that it is an Italian-American invention. My friend Arthur Schwartz, host of WOR Radio's Food Talk with Arthur Schwartz, *is an expert on Neapolitan cooking, as well as historical New York City cooking, and he agrees with me. Arthur believes it was probably developed in a New York Italian restaurant some years ago, and it has been popular ever since. The name refers to the spicy tomato sauce in which the lobster is cooked. Serve this with spaghetti or toasted bread rubbed with garlic.*

2 live lobsters, about 1¼ pounds each

⅓ cup olive oil

2 large garlic cloves, lightly crushed

Pinch of crushed red pepper

1 cup dry white wine

1 (28-ounce) can peeled tomatoes, drained and chopped

6 fresh basil leaves, torn into bits

Salt

1. Place one of the lobsters on a cutting board with the cavity facing up. Do not remove the bands that keep the claws shut. Protect your hand with a heavy towel or pot holder and hold the lobster above the tail. Plunge the tip of a heavy chef's knife into the body where the tail joins the chest. Cut all the way through, separating the tail from the rest of the body. Use poultry shears to remove the thin shell that covers the tail meat. Pull out and remove the dark vein in the tail, but leave the green tomalley and red coral, if any. Repeat with the second lobster. Cut the tail crosswise into 3 or 4 pieces. Set the tail pieces aside. Cut the lobster bodies and claws at the joints into 1- to 2-inch chunks. Smack the claws with the blunt side of the knife to crack them.

2. In a large heavy saucepan, heat the oil over medium heat. Add all the lobster pieces except the tails and cook, stirring often, for 10 minutes. Scatter the garlic and hot pepper around the pieces. Add the wine and cook 1 minute.

3. Add the tomatoes, basil, and salt. Bring to a simmer. Cook, stirring occasionally, until the tomatoes are thickened, about 25

minutes. Add the lobster tails and cook 5 to 10 minutes more or until the tail meat is firm and opaque. Serve immediately.

Baked Stuffed Lobster

Aragoste Amollicate

Makes 4 servings

In Italy, and throughout Europe, the typical lobster variety is the spiny or rock lobster, which lacks the large meaty claws of North American lobsters. Their flavor is very good, though, and they are often sold here as frozen lobster tails. If you don't want to deal with live lobsters, you can make this recipe with frozen tails, reducing the amount of bread crumbs slightly and cooking them without thawing, just until they are opaque in the center. This recipe is typical of Sardinia, though it is eaten all over southern Italy.

4 live lobsters (about 1¼ pounds each)

1 cup plain dry bread crumbs

2 tablespoons chopped fresh flat-leaf parsley

1 garlic clove, finely chopped

Salt and freshly ground black pepper

Olive oil

1 lemon, cut into wedges

1. Place one of the lobsters on a cutting board with the cavity facing up. Do not remove the bands that keep the claws shut. Protect your hand with a heavy towel or pot holder and hold the lobster above the tail. Plunge the tip of a heavy chef's knife into the body where the tail joins the chest. Cut all the way through, separating the tail from the rest of the body. Use poultry shears to remove the thin white shell that covers the underside of the tail and expose the meat. Pull out and remove the dark vein in the tail, but leave the green tomalley and red coral, if any.

2. Place a rack in the center of the oven. Preheat the oven to 450°F. Oil 1 or 2 large roasting pans. Arrange the lobsters on their backs in the baking pans.

3. In a medium bowl, stir together the bread crumbs, parsley, garlic, and salt and pepper to taste. Add 3 tablespoons of oil, or just enough to moisten the crumbs. Scatter the mixture over the lobsters in the pan. Drizzle with a little more oil.

4. Bake the lobsters 12 to 15 minutes, or until the tail meat looks just opaque when cut in the thickest part and feels firm when pressed.

5. Serve immediately with the lemon wedges.

Scallops with Garlic and Parsley

Capesante Aglio e Olio

Makes 4 servings

Sweet fresh scallops cook quickly, perfect for a weeknight meal. This recipe comes from Grado on the Adriatic Coast. I like to use large sea scallops, but smaller bay scallops can be substituted.

¼ cup olive oil

2 garlic cloves, finely chopped

2 tablespoons chopped fresh flat-leaf parsley

1 pound large sea scallops, rinsed and patted dry

Salt and freshly ground black pepper

1 lemon, cut into wedges

1. Pour the oil into a large skillet. Add the garlic, parsley, and hot pepper and cook over medium heat until lightly golden, about 2 minutes.

2. Add the scallops and salt and pepper to taste. Cook, stirring, until the scallops are just barely opaque in the center, about 3 minutes. Serve hot with lemon wedges.

Grilled Scallops and Shrimp

Frutti di Mare alla Griglia

Makes 4 servings

A simple lemon sauce dresses grilled shrimp and scallops. Chunks of firm-fleshed fish such as salmon or swordfish can be substituted.

³⁄₄ pound large sea scallops, rinsed and patted dry

³⁄₄ pound large shrimp, shelled and deveined

Fresh or dried bay leaves

1 medium red onion, cut into 1 inch pieces

¹⁄₄ cup olive oil

2 tablespoons fresh lemon juice

1 tablespoon chopped fresh flat-leaf parsley

¹⁄₂ teaspoon dried oregano, crumbled

Salt and freshly ground black pepper

1. Place a barbecue grill or broiler rack about 5 inches away from the heat source. Preheat the grill or broiler.

2. Thread the scallops and shrimp alternately with the bay leaves and pieces of onion on 8 wood or metal skewers.

3. In a small bowl, whisk together the oil, lemon juice, parsley, oregano, and salt and pepper to taste. Transfer about two-thirds of the sauce mixture to a separate bowl. Reserve. Brush the shellfish with the remaining third of the sauce.

4. Grill or broil until the shrimp are pink and the scallops are lightly browned on one side, about 3 to 4 minutes. Turn over the skewers and cook, until the shrimp are pink and the scallops are lightly browned on the other side, about 3 to 4 minutes more. The shrimp and scallop meat will be just barely opaque in the center. Transfer to a plate and drizzle with the remaining sauce.

Clams and Mussels Posillipo

Vongole e Cozze in Salsa Piccante

Makes 4 servings

Posillipo *is the name of a point of land on the Bay of Naples. It also evokes this dish of fresh clams and mussels in a spicy tomato sauce in the minds of many Italian-Americans. Probably named by a homesick restaurateur in the United States, the recipe seems to have gone out of style, though it is so good it deserves a comeback.*

Serve these in deep bowls over slices of toasted bread or freselle—*hard, black pepper biscuits available in Italian markets.*

3 dozen small hard-shell clams

2 pounds mussels

⅓ cup olive oil

1 tablespoon finely chopped garlic

Pinch of crushed red pepper

½ cup dry white wine

1 (28-ounce) can peeled tomatoes, drained and chopped

1 teaspoon dried oregano, crumbled

Salt and freshly ground black pepper

¼ cup chopped fresh flat-leaf parsley

Italian bread slices, toasted, or freselle

1. Soak the clams and mussels and clams in cold water 30 minutes. Scrub the clams under cold running water with a stiff brush. Cut or pull off the beards from the mussels. Discard any clams or mussels with cracked shells or that refuse to close tightly when touched.

2. Pour the oil into a large heavy pot. Add the garlic and hot pepper. Cook over medium heat until the garlic is lightly golden, about 2 minutes. Add the wine and cook 1 minute more. Stir in the tomatoes. oregano, and salt and pepper to taste. Bring to a simmer and cook 15 minutes.

3. Add the clams and mussels to the pot and cover tightly. Cook until the shells open, about 5 minutes.

4. Place slices of Italian bread in the bottom of 4 pasta bowls. Spoon on the clams and mussels. Sprinkle with chopped parsley and serve immediately.

Baked Stuffed Clams

Vongole Arraganati

Makes 4 servings

Tasty little clams dusted with crunchy seasoned bread crumbs are a favorite all over southern Italy. I like to make these with small to medium clams. If only larger clams are available, chop up the clam meat before topping them with the crumb mixture.

These can be served as an antipasto, but I often make a whole meal of them.

4 dozen small hard-shell clams

½ cup water

½ cup plain dry bread crumbs, preferably homemade

¼ cup freshly grated Parmigiano-Reggiano or Pecorino Romano

¼ cup chopped fresh flat-leaf parsley

1 garlic clove, finely chopped

Salt and freshly ground black pepper

About ⅓ cup extra-virgin olive oil

1 lemon, cut into wedges

1. Soak the clams in cold water 30 minutes. Scrub with a brush under cold running water. Discard any with cracked shells or that do not close tightly when touched.

2. Place the clams in a large pot with the water. Cover and bring to a simmer. After about 5 minutes, remove the clams as they open and place them in a bowl. Discard clams that don't open.

3. Pour the clam juices into a bowl. Remove the clams from their shells and rinse each one in the liquid to remove any sand. Separate the shell halves. Place half the shells on a large baking sheet. Place a clam in each shell. Strain the clam juice through a paper coffee filter or dampened cheesecloth into a bowl. Spoon a little of the juice on each clam.

4. Preheat the broiler. In a medium bowl, combine the bread crumbs, cheese, parsley, garlic, and salt and pepper to taste. Add enough oil to moisten the crumbs. Spoon a small amount of the crumbs loosely on top of each clam. Do not pack the crumbs down.

5. Broil 4 minutes or until the crumbs are lightly browned. Serve hot with lemon wedges.

Mussels with Black Pepper

Impepata di Cozze

Makes 4 to 6 servings

Inexpensive and widely available, mussels are great in pasta, soups, or stews. The only problem is cleaning them, as wild mussels can require a lot of attention. Farm-raised mussels are the exception. Though they are not as tasty as wild mussels, they are much cleaner and there is less waste from damaged mussels. This recipe has a tangy flavor from the wine, lemon juice, and an unusually large amount of black pepper. It is a classic recipe from Naples.

6 pounds mussels

½ cup olive oil

6 garlic cloves, finely chopped

½ cup chopped fresh flat-leaf parsley

1 tablespoon freshly ground black pepper

1 cup dry white wine

1 tablespoon fresh lemon juice

1. Soak the mussels in cold water 30 minutes. Cut or pull off the beards. Discard any mussels with cracked shells or that do not close tightly when touched.

2. Pour the oil into a large pot. Add the garlic. Cook over medium heat until golden, about 1 minute. Stir in the parsley and pepper. Add the mussels, wine, and lemon juice to the pot. Cover and cook, shaking the pan occasionally, until the mussels begin to open, about 5 minutes.

3. Transfer the opened mussels to serving bowls. Cook any mussels that remain closed a minute or two longer. Discard any that do not open. Pour the cooking liquid over the mussels. Serve hot.

Mussels with Garlic and White Wine

Cozze agli Aromi

Makes 4 servings

Instead of serving them with bread, these mussels can be tossed with hot cooked spaghetti. Small hard-shell clams can be substituted for the mussels.

4 pounds mussels

¼ cup olive oil

2 garlic cloves, chopped

2 green onions, chopped

2 sprigs fresh thyme

2 tablespoons chopped fresh flat-leaf parsley

1 bay leaf

1 cup dry white wine

Italian bread slices, toasted

1. Soak the mussels in cold water 30 minutes. Cut or pull off the beards. Discard any mussels with cracked shells or that do not close tightly when touched.

2. Pour the oil into a large saucepan. Add the garlic, green onions, thyme, parsley, and bay leaf. Cook over medium heat until the onions are tender, about 2 minutes.

3. Add the mussels and wine. Cover and cook, shaking the pan occasionally, about 5 minutes or until the mussels begin to open.

4. Transfer the opened mussels to individual serving bowls. Cook any mussels that remain closed a minute or two longer; discard any that do not open. Simmer the liquid 1 minute more and pour it over the mussels. Serve hot with toasted bread.

Sardinian Mussels with Saffron

Cozze allo Zafferano

Makes 4 servings

Saffron, a spice made from the stigmas of crocus flowers, adds an exotic flavor and beautiful color to these mussels. Though much of the world's saffron comes from Spain, it is also produced in the Abruzzo region of Italy. When buying saffron, always buy whole threads, which keep their flavor longer. Look for deep red-orange color. The darker color is an indication of better quality.

1 teaspoon saffron threads

1 cup dry white wine

4 pounds mussels

1 medium onion, finely chopped

⅓ cup olive oil

1 cup peeled, seeded, and chopped ripe tomatoes

6 basil leaves, torn into bits

2 tablespoons chopped fresh flat-leaf parsley

1. Soak the saffron in the white wine for 10 minutes. Meanwhile, soak the mussels in cold water for 30 minutes. Cut or pull off the beards. Discard any mussels with cracked shells or that do not close tightly when touched.

2. In a large saucepan, cook the onion in the oil over medium heat until golden, about 10 minutes. Add the saffron, wine, and tomatoes and bring to a simmer. Stir in the basil and parsley.

3. Add the mussels and cover the pan. Cook, shaking the pan occasionally, about 5 minutes or until the mussels begin to open.

4. Transfer the opened mussels to individual serving bowls. Cook any mussels that remain closed a minute or two longer; discard any that do not open. Simmer the liquid 1 minute more and pour it over the mussels. Serve hot.

DESSERTS

Almond Cream Cups

Biscuit Tortoni

Makes 8 servings

When I was growing up, this was the standard Italian restaurant dessert, something like tiramisù has been for the last 15 years or so. Though it may be out of fashion, it is still delicious and easy to make.

If you want a more elegant-looking dessert, spoon the mixture into parfait glasses or ramekins. The maraschino cherries add a touch of color, but you can leave them out if you prefer.

2 cups chilled heavy or whipping cream

½ cup confectioners' sugar

2 teaspoons pure vanilla extract

½ teaspoon almond extract

2 egg whites, at room temperature

Pinch of salt

8 maraschino cherries, drained and chopped (optional)

2 tablespoons finely chopped toasted almonds

12 to 16 imported Italian amaretti cookies, finely crushed (about 1 cup crumbs)

1. At least 20 minutes before you are ready to whip the cream, place a large bowl and the beaters of an electric mixer in the refrigerator. Line a muffin tin with 8 pleated paper or foil cupcake liners.

2. Remove the bowl and beaters from the refrigerator. Pour the cream, sugar, and extracts into the bowl and whip the mixture at high speed until it holds its shape softly when the beaters are lifted, about 4 minutes. Refrigerate the whipped cream.

3. In a large clean bowl with clean beaters, whip the egg whites with the salt on low speed until foamy. Gradually increase the speed and beat until the whites hold soft peaks when the beaters are lifted. With a flexible spatula, gently fold the whites into the whipped cream.

4. Set aside 2 tablespoons of the amaretti crumbs. Fold the remaining crumbs, the cherries, and the almonds into the cream mixture. Spoon into the prepared muffin cups. Sprinkle with the reserved amaretti crumbs.

5. Cover with foil and freeze at least 4 hours or up to overnight. Remove from the refrigerator 15 minutes before serving.

Orange Spumone

Spumone di Arancia

Makes 6 servings

Spumone comes from spuma, meaning "foam." It has a creamier texture than regular gelato because the egg yolks are cooked with the hot sugar syrup to make a thick custard. Though it is rich with egg yolks, it is light and airy from the egg foam and whipped cream.

3 navel oranges

1 cup water

¾ cup sugar

6 large egg yolks

1 cup chilled heavy or whipping cream

1. Grate the zest from the oranges and squeeze the juice. (There should be 3 tablespoons of the zest and $2/3$ cup of juice.)

2. In a medium saucepan, combine the water and sugar. Bring to a simmer over medium heat, then cook, stirring occasionally, until the sugar dissolves.

3. In a large heatproof bowl, whisk the egg yolks until blended. Slowly add the hot sugar syrup in a thin stream, whisking constantly. Pour the mixture into the saucepan and cook over low heat, stirring with a wooden spoon, until slightly thickened and the mixture lightly coats the spoon.

4. Pour the mixture through a fine-mesh strainer into a bowl. Stir in the orange juice and zest. Let cool, then cover and refrigerate until chilled, at least 1 hour. Place a large bowl and the beaters of an electric mixer in the refrigerator.

5. Just before serving, remove the bowl and beaters from the refrigerator. Pour the cream into the bowl and whip the cream at high speed until it holds its shape softly when the beaters are lifted, about 4 minutes. With a flexible spatula, gently fold the cream into orange mixture.

6. Freeze in an ice-cream freezer according to the manufacturer's instructions. Pack into a container, cover, and freeze. Serve within 24 hours.

Almond Semifreddo

Semifreddo alle Mandorle

Makes 8 servings

Semifreddo means "half-cold." This dessert got its name because though it is frozen, its texture stays soft and creamy. It melts easily, so have everything very cold while you make it. Warm Chocolate Sauce is a good accompaniment.

¾ cup chilled heavy or whipping cream

1 teaspoon pure vanilla extract

¾ cup sugar

¼ cup water

4 large eggs, at room temperature

6 amaretti cookies, finely crushed

2 tablespoons toasted almonds, finely chopped

2 tablespoons sliced almonds

1. Line a 9 × 5 × 3–inch metal loaf pan with plastic wrap, leaving a 2-inch overhang on the ends. Chill the pan in the freezer. At least 20 minutes before you are ready to whip the cream, place a large bowl and the beaters of an electric mixer in the refrigerator.

2. When ready, remove the bowl and beaters from the refrigerator. Pour the cream and vanilla into the bowl and whip the cream at high speed until it holds its shape softly when the beaters are lifted, about 4 minutes. Return the bowl to the refrigerator.

3. In a small saucepan, combine the sugar and water. Bring to a simmer over medium heat, then cook, stirring occasionally, until the sugar is completely dissolved, about 2 minutes.

4. In a large mixer bowl, beat the eggs with the mixer on medium speed until foamy, about 1 minute. Slowly beat the hot sugar syrup into the eggs in a thin stream. Continue beating until the mixture is very light and fluffy and feels cool to the touch, 8 to 10 minutes.

5. With a flexible spatula, gently fold the whipped cream into the egg mixture. Gently fold in the cookie crumbs and chopped almonds.

6. Scrape the mixture into the prepared loaf pan. Cover securely with the plastic wrap and freeze 4 hours up to overnight.

7. Unwrap the pan. Invert a serving plate on top of the pan. Holding the plate and pan together, invert them both. Lift off the pan and carefully remove the plastic wrap. Sprinkle with the sliced almonds.

8. Cut into slices and serve immediately.

Florentine Frozen Dome Cake

Zuccotto

Makes 8 servings

Inspired by the dome of the beautiful Duomo, the cathedral in the heart of Florence, this impressive dessert is actually quite easy to make, partly because it uses prepared cake.

1 (12-ounce) pound cake

2 tablespoons rum

2 tablespoons orange liqueur

Filling

1 pint heavy or whipping cream

¼ cup confectioner's sugar, plus more for garnish

1 teaspoon pure vanilla extract

4 ounces semisweet chocolate, finely chopped

2 tablespoons sliced almonds, toasted and cooled

Fresh berries (optional)

1. At least 20 minutes before you are ready to whip the cream, place a large bowl and the beaters of an electric mixer in the refrigerator. Line a 2-quart round bowl or mold with plastic wrap. Cut the cake into slices no more than $1/4$-inch thick. Cut each slice in half diagonally, forming two triangular pieces, and lay them all on a platter.

2. In a small bowl, mix together the rum and liqueur, and sprinkle the mixture over the cake. Place as many cake pieces as needed side by side—pointed-side down—in the bowl to form one layer. Cover the remaining inside surface of the bowl with the remaining cake, cutting the pieces to fit as needed. Fill in any gaps with cut-up pieces of cake. Set aside the remaining cake for the top.

3. Prepare the filling: Remove the bowl and beaters from the refrigerator. Pour the cream into the bowl. Add the confectioners' sugar and vanilla. Whip at high speed until the cream holds its shape softly when the beaters are lifted, about 4 minutes. Gently fold in the chocolate and almonds.

4. Spoon the cream mixture into the mold, being careful not to disturb the cake. Place the remaining cake slices in a layer on top. Cover securely with plastic wrap and freeze the mold 4 hours up to overnight.

5. To serve, remove the plastic wrap and invert a serving plate on top of the bowl. Holding the plate and bowl together, invert them both. Lift off the bowl. Remove the plastic wrap and sprinkle with confectioner's sugar. Place the berries around the cake. Cut into wedges to serve.

Honeyed Mascarpone Sauce

Salsina di Mascarpone

Makes 2 cups

Serve this on fresh berries or on Marsala Walnut Cake.

$\frac{1}{2}$ cup mascarpone

3 tablespoons honey

$\frac{1}{2}$ teaspoon grated lemon zest

1 cup chilled heavy cream, whipped

In a large bowl, whisk the mascarpone, honey, and lemon zest until smooth. Fold in the whipped cream. Serve immediately.

Fresh Strawberry Sauce

Salsina di Fragole

Makes 1½ cups

Raspberries can also be prepared this way. If you do use raspberries, strain the sauce to eliminate the seeds.

1 pint fresh strawberries, rinsed and hulled

3 tablespoons sugar, or to taste

¼ cup fresh orange juice

2 tablespoons orange liqueur, cassis, or light rum

In a food processor or blender, combine all of the ingredients. Puree until smooth. Serve or transfer to an airtight container and store in the refrigerator up to 24 hours.

Warm Berry Sauce

Salsina Calda di Frutti di Bosco

Makes about 2½ cups

This sauce is excellent on lemon, mascarpone, cinnamon, or "cream" ice cream or plain cake.

4 cups mixed fresh berries, such as blueberries, strawberries, raspberries, and blackberries

¼ cup water

¼ cup sugar or more

1. Rinse the berries and remove the hulls or stems. Cut the strawberries into halves or quarters if they are large.

2. In a medium saucepan, combine the berries, water, and sugar. Bring to a simmer over medium heat. Cook, stirring occasionally, until the berries are soft and the juices are slightly thickened, about 5 minutes. Taste and add more sugar, if necessary. Remove from the heat and let cool slightly. Serve or transfer to an airtight container and store in the refrigerator up to 24 hours.

Year-Round Raspberry Sauce

Salsa di Lampone

Makes about 2 cups

Even when berries are not in season, you can still make a delicious fresh-tasting sauce. The raspberry flavor and color goes especially well with almond- and chocolate-flavored desserts and cakes. For a simple but beautiful dessert, pour this sauce, and a few fresh berries, too, over thin slices of cantaloupe.

The sauce can also be made with frozen blueberries or strawberries or a combination of berries. If you can't find berries in syrup, use unsweetened fruit and add sugar to taste.

2 (10-ounce) packages frozen raspberries in syrup, partially thawed

1 teaspoon cornstarch mixed with 2 tablespoons water

About 1 teaspoon fresh lemon juice

1. Pass the berries through a food mill fitted with a fine blade, or puree them in a food processor and press them through a fine-mesh strainer.

2. Bring the puree to a simmer in a small saucepan. Stir in the cornstarch mixture and cook, stirring frequently, until slightly thickened, about 1 minute. Stir in the lemon juice. Let cool slightly. Serve or transfer to an airtight container and store in the refrigerator up to 3 days.

Warm Chocolate Sauce

Salsa Calda al Cioccolato

Makes about 1½ cups

Espresso intensifies the chocolate flavor of this delicious sauce, but you can leave it out if you prefer. Serve with ice cream, semifreddo, or plain cakes; it goes with a wide variety of desserts.

8 ounces bittersweet or semisweet chocolate, chopped

1 cup heavy cream

Place the chocolate and cream in the top of a double boiler or in a heatproof bowl set over a pan of simmering water. Let stand until the chocolate is softened. Stir until smooth. Serve warm or transfer to an airtight container and store in the refrigerator up to 3 days. Reheat gently.

Warm Mocha Sauce: Stir in 1 teaspoon instant espresso powder with the chocolate.

Ladyfingers

Savoiardi

Makes 4 dozen

These crisp, light cookies, called Savoiardi, are named for the royal house of Savoy that ruled the region of Piedmont from the fifteenth century and all of Italy from 1861 up until World War II. They are perfect tea cookies and are excellent with ice cream or fruit, but they can also be used in composed desserts like tiramisù.

Potato starch is used to make the cookies crisp and light. You can find potato starch in many supermarkets, or you can substitute cornstarch.

4 large eggs, at room temperature

⅔ cup sugar

2 teaspoons pure vanilla extract

½ cup all-purpose flour

¼ cup potato starch

Pinch of salt

1. Preheat the oven to 400°F. Grease and flour 3 large baking sheets.

2. Separate the eggs. In a large bowl, using an electric mixer at medium speed, beat the egg yolks with $^1/_3$ cup of the sugar and the vanilla until thick and pale yellow, about 7 minutes.

3. In a large clean bowl with clean beaters, beat the egg whites with a pinch of salt on low speed until foamy. Increase the speed to high and gradually add the remaining $^1/_3$ cup sugar. Beat until the egg whites hold soft peaks when the beaters are lifted, about 5 minutes.

4. With a rubber spatula, fold about $^1/_3$ of the egg whites into the egg yolks to lighten them. Gradually fold in the remaining whites.

5. Place the flour and starch in a small fine-mesh strainer. Shake the strainer over the eggs and fold in the dry ingredients gently but thoroughly.

6. Scoop the batter into a large pastry bag fitted with a $^1/_2$-inch tip or into a heavy-duty plastic bag with a corner cut off. (Do not fill the bag more than halfway.) Pipe the batter onto the baking sheets, forming 3 × 1–inch logs about 1 inch apart.

7. Have several wire cooling racks ready. Bake the cookies 10 to 12 minutes, or until they are golden brown and feel firm when touched lightly in the center.

8. Transfer the baking sheets to the cooling racks. Cool the cookies 2 minutes on the baking sheets, then transfer them to the racks to cool completely. Store in an airtight container at room temperature up to 2 weeks.

Lightning Source UK Ltd.
Milton Keynes UK
UKHW020644240521
384271UK00011B/761